Charles Robinson, Eugene Field, Kenneth Grahame, America Project
Making of

Lullaby-Land

Songs of Childhood

Charles Robinson, Eugene Field, Kenneth Grahame, America Project Making of

Lullaby-Land
Songs of Childhood

ISBN/EAN: 9783744712682

Printed in Europe, USA, Canada, Australia, Japan

Cover: Foto ©Thomas Meinert / pixelio.de

More available books at **www.hansebooks.com**

LULLABY-LAND.

Songs of Childhood.

by

EUGENE FIELD.

Selected by KENNETH GRAHAME, and illustrated by CHARLES ROBINSON.

18 97

NEW YORK
CHARLES SCRIBNER'S SONS
· LONDON ·
JOHN · LANE

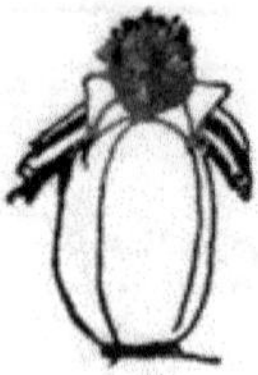

Lullaby-land.

LULLABY-
LAND.

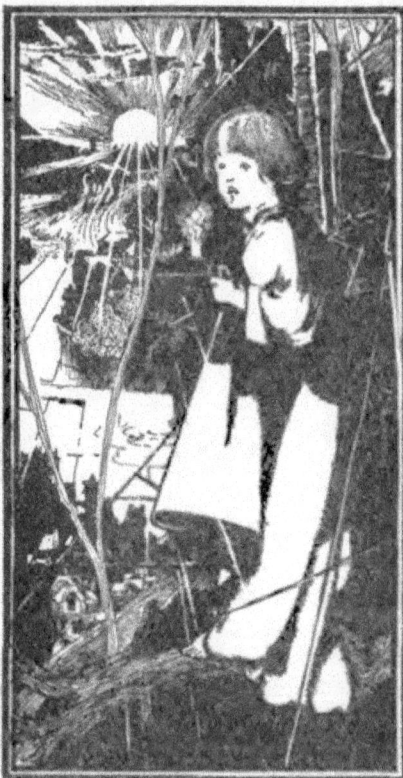

Preface.

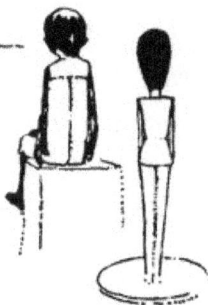

There is a sort of a garden —
or rather an estate, of park
and fallow and waste — nay,
perhaps we may call it a kingdom, albeit a
noman's-land and an everyman's land — which
lies so close to the frontier of our work-a-day
world that a step will take us therein. Indeed,

7

*some will have it that we are there all the time,
that it is the real fourth dimension, and that at
any moment — if we did but know the trick — we
might find ourselves trotting along its pleasant
alleys, without once quitting our arm-chair.
Nonsense-Land is one of the names painted up
on the board at the frontier-station; and there
the custom-house officers are very strict. You
may take as much tobacco as you please, any
quantity of spirits, and fripperies of every sort,
new and old; but all common-sense, all logic,
all serious argument, must strictly be declared,
and is promptly confiscated. Once safely across
the border, it is with no surprise at all that
you greet the Lead Soldier strutting somewhat
stiffly to meet you, the Dog with eyes as big as
mill-wheels following affably at his heel; on
the banks of the streams little Johnny-head-in-
air is perpetually being hauled out of the water;
while the plaintive voice of the Gryphon is
borne inland from the margin of the sea.*

*Most people, at one time or another, have
travelled in this delectable country, if only in
young and irresponsible days. Certain un-
fortunates, unequipped by nature for a voyage*

*in such latitudes, have never visited it at all,
and assuredly never will. A happy few never
quit it entirely at any time. Domiciled in that
pleasant atmosphere, they peep into the world of
facts but fitfully, at moments; and decline to
sacrifice their high privilege of citizenship at
any summons to a low conformity.*

*Of this fortunate band was Eugene Field.
He knew the country thoroughly, its highways
and its byways alike. Its language was the
one he was fondest of talking; and he always
refused to emigrate and to settle down anywhere
else. As soon as he set himself to narrate the
goings-on there, those of us who had been
tourists in bygone days, but had lost our
return-tickets, pricked up our ears, and listened,
and remembered, and knew. The Dinkey-Bird,
we recollected at once, had been singing, the day
we left, in the amfalula-tree; and there, of
course, he must have been singing ever since,
only we had forgotten the way to listen.
Eugene Field gently reminded us, and the
Dinkey-Bird was vocal once more, to be silent
never again. Shut-Eye Train had been starting
every night with the utmost punctuality; it was*

we who had long ago lost our way to the booking-office (I really do not know the American for booking-office). Now we can hurry up the platform whenever we please, and hear the doors slam and the whistle toot as we sink back on those first-class cushions! And the Chocolate Cat,— why, of course the cats were all chocolate then! And how pleasantly brittle their tails were, and how swiftly, though culled and sucked each day, they sprouted afresh!

It is an engaging theory, that we are all of us just as well informed as the great philosophers, poets, wits, who are getting all the glory; only unfortunately our memories are not equally good— we forget, we forget so terribly! Those belauded gentlemen, termed by our fathers " makers "— creators, to wit — they are only reminders *after all: flappers, Gulliver would have called them. The parched peas in their gaily-painted bladders rattle with reminiscences as they flap us on the ears; and at once we recall what we are rightly abashed beyond measure to have for one instant forgotten. At any rate, it is only when the writer comes along who strikes a new clear note, who does a*

thing both true and fresh, that we say to our-
selves, not only "How I wish I had done that
myself!"—but also "And I would have done
it, too—if only I had remembered it in time!"
Perhaps this is one of the tests of originality.

Of course I am touching upon but one side of
Eugene Field the writer. An American of
Americans, much of his verse was devoted to
the celebration of what we may call the minor
joys which go to make social happiness in the
life he lived with so frank and rounded a com-
pletion—a celebration which appealed to his
countrymen no less keenly, that the joys were of
a sort which, perhaps from some false sense of
what makes fitness in subject, had hitherto
lacked their poet—on that side at least. This,
of course, was the fault of the poets. And
though I spoke just now of minor joys, there
are really no such things as minor joys—or
minor thrushes and blackbirds. Fortunately
this other aspect does not need to be considered
here. I say fortunately, because it is not
given to a writer to know more than one
Land—to know it intimately, that is to say, so
as to dare to write about it. This is the Law

*and the Prophets. Even that most native
utterance, which sings of "the clink of the ice
in the pitcher that the boy brings up the hall,"
appeals to us but faintly, at second-hand. That
pitcher does not clink in England.*

*In this spheral existence all straight lines,
sufficiently prolonged, prove to be circles: and
a line of thought is no exception. We are
back at the point we started from — the con-
sideration of Eugene Field as a citizen; of a
sort of a cloud-country, to start with; and
later, of a land more elemental. In either
capacity we find the same note, of the joy of life.
We find the same honest resolve, to accept the
rules and to play out the game accordingly; the
same conviction, that the game is in itself a
good one, well worth the playing. And so,
with no misgiving, he takes his America with
just the same heartiness as his Nonsense-
land.*

*The little boy who should by rights have
been lost in the forest, by the white pebbles he
had warily dropped found his way back safely
to sunlight and to home; and to keep in touch
with earth is at least to ensure progression in*

*temperate and sweet-breathed atmosphere, as
well as in a certain zone, and that no narrow
one, of appreciation; the appreciation of our
fellows, the world over; those who, whatever
their hemisphere, daily find themselves pricked
by a common sun, with the same stimulus for
every cuticle, towards pleasures surprisingly
similar.*

KENNETH GRAHAME.

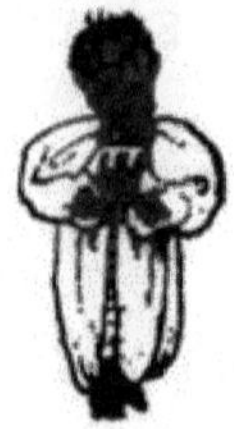

CONTENTS

From "Love-Songs of Childhood"

CONTENTS

From "With Trumpet and Drum."

16

CONTENTS

From "The Second Book of Verse."

From "The Lonesome little Shoe."
in "The Holy Cross and Other Tales."

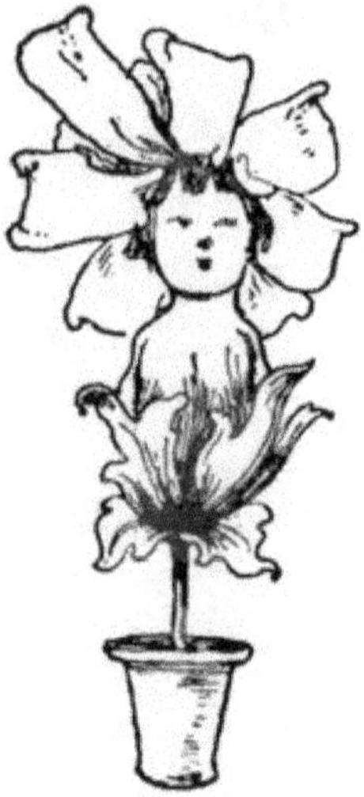

* * * * * *

The Rock-a-by Lady.

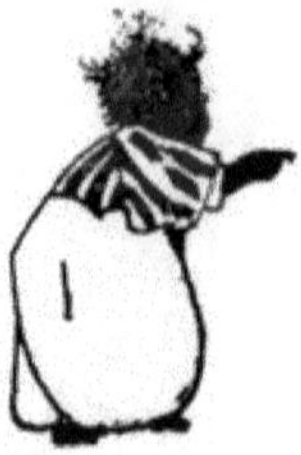

THE ROCK-A-
BY LADY

THE Rock-a-By Lady from Hushaby street
    Comes stealing; comes creeping;
The poppies they hang from her head to her feet,

And each hath a dream that is tiny and fleet—
She bringeth her poppies to you, my sweet,
　　When she findeth you sleeping!

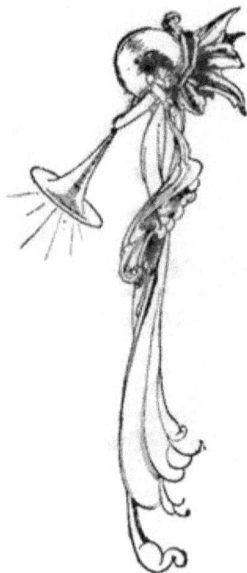

There is one little dream of a beautiful drum—
　　"Rub-a-dub!" it goeth;
There is one little dream of a big sugar-plum,

"THERE IS ONE LITTLE DREAM
OF A BEAUTIFUL DRUM" —

And lo! thick and fast the other dreams come
Of popguns that bang, and tin tops that hum,
    And a trumpet that bloweth!

And dollies peep out of those wee little dreams
        With laughter and singing;
And boats go a-floating on silvery streams,
And the stars peek-a-boo with their own misty
        gleams,

And up, up, and up, where the Mother Moon
    beams,
    The fairies go winging!

Would you dream all these dreams that are tiny
    and fleet?
    They'll come to you sleeping;
So shut the two eyes that are weary, my sweet,
For the Rock-a-By Lady from Hushaby street,
With poppies that hang from her head to her
    feet,
    Comes stealing; comes creeping.

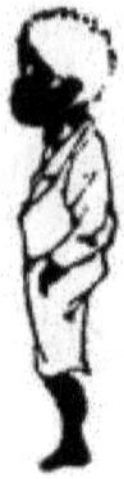

Garden
and Cradle.

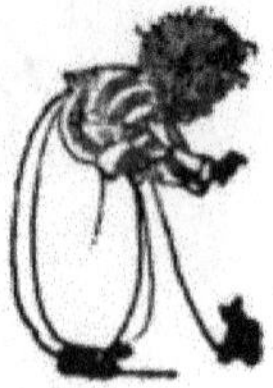

GARDEN
AND CRADLE

WHEN our babe he goeth walking in his
    garden,
Around his tinkling feet the sunbeams play;

The posies they are good to him,
And bow them as they should to him,
As fareth he upon his kingly way;
And birdlings of the wood to him
Make music, gentle music, all the day,
When our babe he goeth walking in his garden.

When our babe he goeth swinging in his cradle,
Then the night it looketh ever sweetly down;
The little stars are kind to him,
The moon she hath a mind to him
And layeth on his head a golden crown;
And singeth then the wind to him
A song, the gentle song of Bethlem-town,
When our babe he goeth swinging in his cradle.

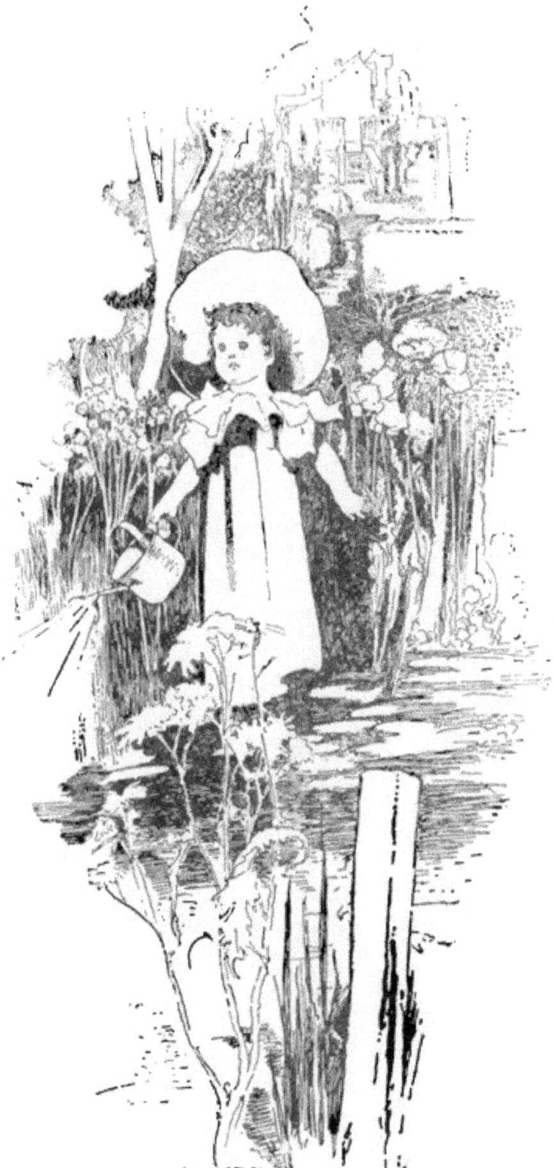

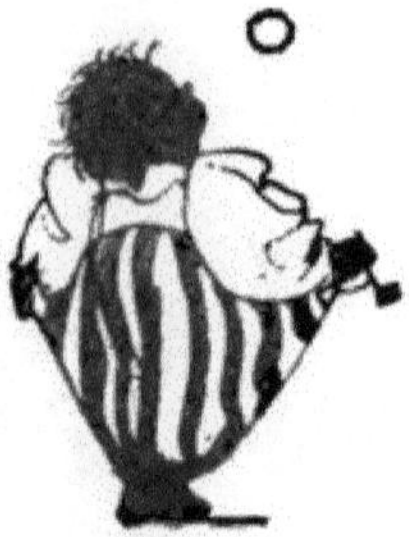

The
Night Wind.

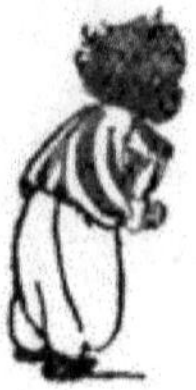

THE NIGHT WIND

HAVE you ever heard the wind go "Yooooo"?
    'Tis a pitiful sound to hear!
It seems to chill you through and through
    With a strange and speechless fear.
'Tis the voice of the night that broods outside
    When folks should be asleep,

THE NIGHT WIND

And many and many 's the time I've cried
To the darkness brooding far and wide
    Over the land and the deep:
" Whom do you want, O lonely night,
    That you wail the long hours through? "
And the night would say in its ghostly way:
        " Yoooooooo!
         Yooooooo!
         Yoooooooo! "

My mother told me long ago
    (When I was a little tad)
That when the night went wailing so,
    Somebody had been bad;
And then, when I was snug in bed,
    Whither I had been sent,
With the blankets pulled up round my head,
I'd think of what my mother 'd said,
    And wonder what boy she meant!
And " Who's been bad to-day? " I'd ask
    Of the wind that hoarsely blew,
And the voice would say in its meaningful way.
        " Yoooooooo!
         Yooooooo!
         Yoooooooo! "

38

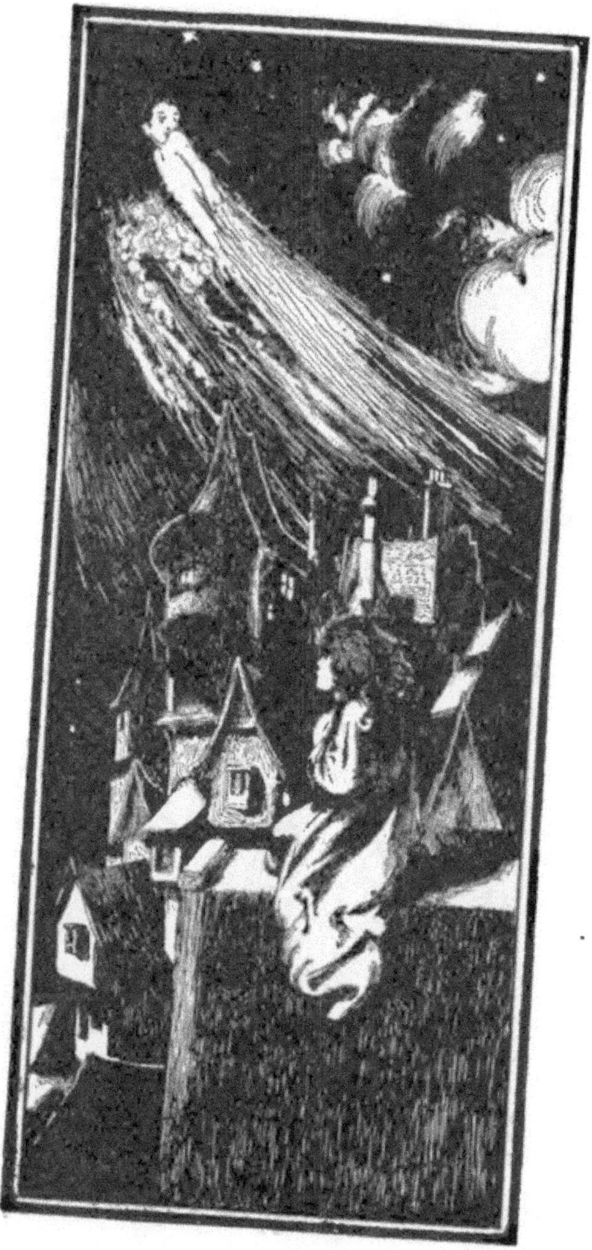

That this was true I must allow —
  You'll not believe it, though!
Yes, though I'm quite a model now,
  I was not always so.
And if you doubt what things I say,
  Suppose you make the test;
Suppose, when you've been bad some day
And up to bed are sent away
  From mother and the rest —
Suppose you ask, "Who has been bad?"
  And then you'll hear what's true;
For the wind will moan in its ruefulest tone:
     "Yoooooooo!
     Yoooooooo!
     Yooooooooo!"

The
Dinkey Bird.

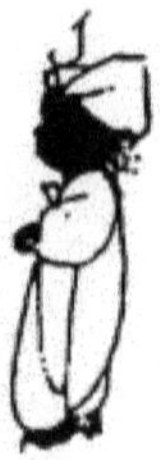

THE DINKEY ᔓ ᔓ ᔓ BIRD.

IN an ocean, 'way out yonder
   (As all sapient people know),

43

THE DINKEY-BIRD

Is the land of Wonder-Wander,
  Whither children love to go;
It's their playing, romping, swinging,
  That give great joy to me
While the Dinkey-Bird goes singing
  In the amfalula tree!

There the gum-drops grow like cherries,
  And taffy's thick as peas —
Caramels you pick like berries
  When, and where, and how you please;
Big red sugar-plums are clinging
  To the cliffs beside that sea
Where the Dinkey-Bird is singing
  In the amfalula tree.

44

THE DINKEY-BIRD

So when children shout and scamper
  And make merry all the day,
When there's naught to put a damper
  To the ardor of their play;
When I hear their laughter ringing,
  Then I'm sure as sure can be
That the Dinkey-Bird is singing
  In the amfalula tree.

For the Dinkey-Bird's bravuras
  And staccatos are so sweet —
His roulades, appoggiaturas,
  And robustos so complete,
That the youth of every nation —
  Be they near or far away —
Have especial delectation
  In that gladsome roundelay.

Their eyes grow bright and brighter,
  Their lungs begin to crow,
Their hearts get light and lighter,
  And their cheeks are all aglow;
For an echo cometh bringing
  The news to all and me,
That the Dinkey-Bird is singing
  In the amfalula tree.

THE DINKEY-BIRD

I'm sure you like to go there
  To see your feathered friend —
And so many goodies grow there
  You would like to comprehend !
Speed, little dreams, your winging
  To that land across the sea
Where the Dinkey-Bird is singing
  In the amfalula tree !

46

So, so,
Rock-a-by so!

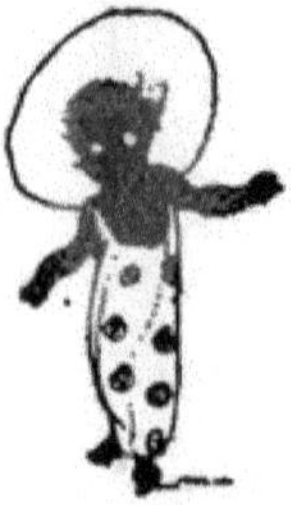

SO, SO, ROCK-A-BY, SO!

SO, so, rock-a-by so!
  Off to the garden where dreamikins grow;
And here is a kiss on your winkyblink eyes,
  And here is a kiss on your dimpledown cheek

SO, SO, ROCK-A-BY SO

And here is a kiss for the treasure that lies
In the beautiful garden way up in the skies
  Which you seek.
Now mind these three kisses wherever you go —
So, so, rock-a-by so!

There's one little fumfay who lives there, I
    know,
For he dances all night where the dreamikins
    grow;
I send him this kiss on your droopydrop eyes,
  I send him this kiss on your rosy-red cheek.
And here is a kiss for the dream that shall rise
When the fumfay shall dance in those far-away
    skies
  Which you seek.
Be sure that you pay those three kisses you
    owe —
So, so, rock-a-by so!

And, by-low, as you rock-a-by go,
Don't forget mother who loveth you so!
And here is her kiss on your weepydeep eyes,
  And here is her kiss on your peachypink
    cheek,

50

And here is her kiss for the dreamland that lies
Like a babe on the breast of those far-away
   skies
  Which you seek —
The blinkywink garden where dreamikins grow —
So, so, rock-a-by so!

The Duel.

THE DUEL.

THE gingham dog and the calico cat
    Side by side on the table sat;
'Twas half-past twelve, and (what do you think!)
Nor one nor t'other had slept a wink!

The old Dutch clock and the Chinese plate
Appeared to know as sure as fate
There was going to be a terrible spat.
   (I wasn't there ; I simply state
   What was told me by the Chinese plate!)

The gingham dog went " bow-wow-wow! "
And the calico cat replied " mee-ow ! "
The air was littered, an hour or so,
With bits of gingham and calico,
   While the old Dutch clock in the chimney
      place
   Up with its hands before its face,
For it always dreaded a family row !
   (Now mind: I'm only telling you
   What the old Dutch clock declares is true!)

The Chinese plate looked very blue,
And wailed, " Oh, dear ! what shall we do? "
But the gingham dog and the calico cat
Wallowed this way and tumbled that,
   Employing every tooth and claw
   In the awfullest way you ever saw —
And, oh ! how the gingham and calico flew !
   (Don't fancy I exaggerate !
   I got my news from the Chinese plate!)

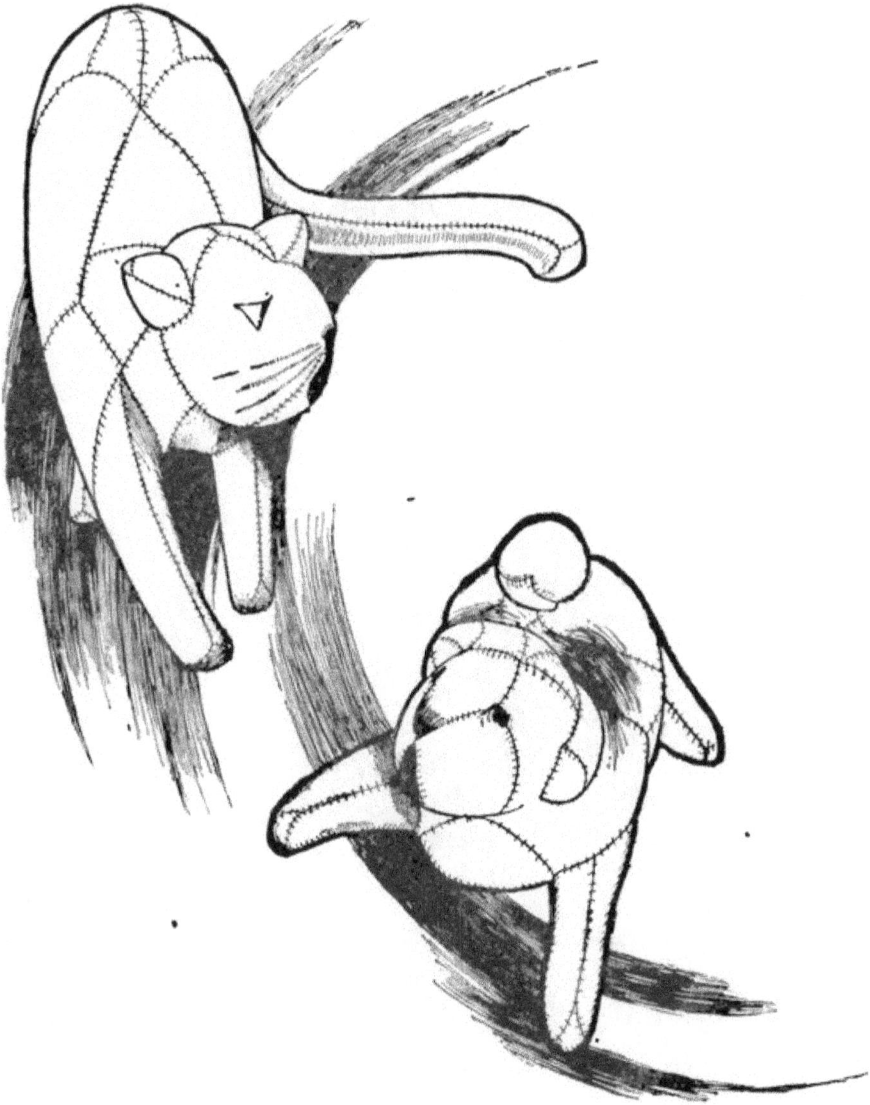

THE DUEL

Next morning, where the two had sat,
They found no trace of dog or cat;
And some folks think unto this day
That burglars stole that pair away!
    But the truth about the cat and pup
    Is this: they ate each other up!
Now what do you really think of that!
    (*The old Dutch clock it told me so,*
    And that is how I came to know.)

Good
Children Street.

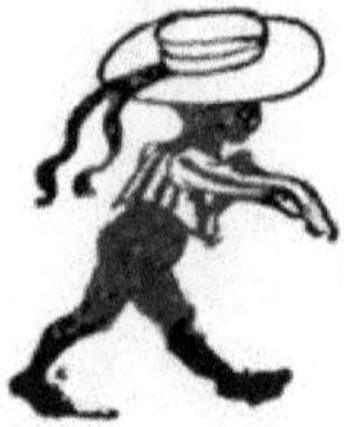

GOOD-CHILDREN STREET.

THERE'S a dear little home in Good-Children street —
My heart turneth fondly to-day
Where tinkle of tongues and patter of feet
Make sweetest of music at play;
Where the sunshine of love illumines each face
And warms every heart in that old-fashioned place.

61

For dear little children go romping about
    With dollies and tin tops and drums,
And, my! how they frolic and scamper and
    shout
    Till bedtime too speedily comes!

Oh, days they are golden and days they are
    fleet
With little folk living in Good-Children street.

See, here comes an army with guns painted red,
    And swords, caps, and plumes of all sorts;
The captain rides gaily and proudly ahead
    On a stick-horse that prances and snorts!
Oh, legions of soldiers you're certain to meet —
Nice make-believe soldiers — in Good-Children
    street.

And yonder Odette wheels her dolly about —
    Poor dolly! I'm sure she is ill,
For one of her blue china eyes has dropped out
    And her voice is asthmatic'ly shrill.
Then, too, I observe she is minus her feet,
Which causes much sorrow in Good-Children
    street.

'Tis so the dear children go romping about
    With dollies and banners and drums,
And I venture to say they are sadly put out

63

When an end to their jubilee comes:
Oh, days they are golden and days they are
    fleet
With little folk living in Good-Children street!

The Bottle Tree.

THE·

BOTTLE TREE.

A BOTTLE TREE bloometh in Winkyway
land —
  Heigh-ho for a bottle, I say!
A snug little berth in that ship I demand
  That rocketh the Bottle-Tree babies away
  Where the Bottle Tree bloometh by night and
    by day
And reacheth its fruit to each wee, dimpled
  hand;

You take of that fruit as much as you list,
For colic 's a nuisance that doesn't exist!

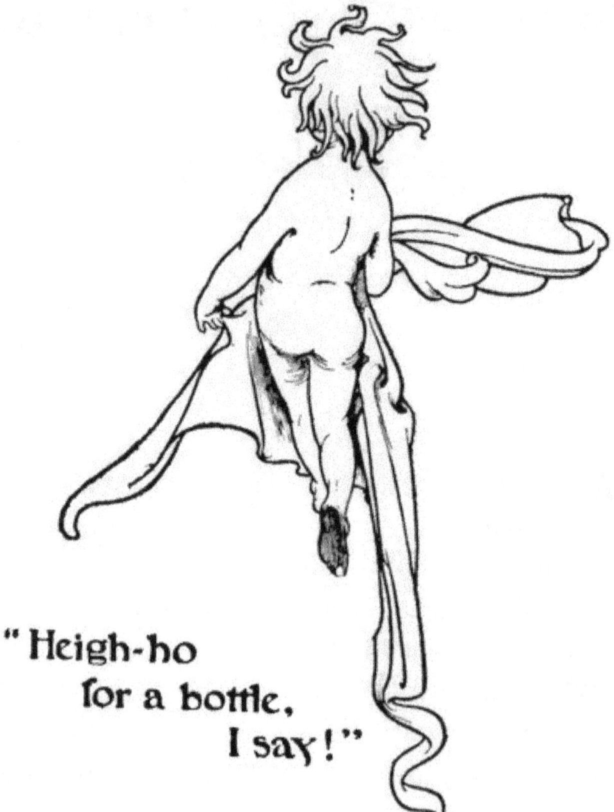

" Heigh-ho
    for a bottle,
        I say!"

So cuddle me close, and cuddle me fast,
    And cuddle me snug in my cradle away,

For I hunger and thirst for that precious repast —
Heigh-ho for a bottle, I say!

". . . of bottle
tree babies
expand."

The Bottle Tree bloometh by night and by day!
Heigh-ho for Winkyway land!

And Bottle-Tree fruit (as I've heard people say)
   Makes bellies of Bottle-Tree babies expand —
   And that is a trick I would fain understand!
Heigh-ho for a bottle to-day!
   And heigh-ho for a bottle to-night —
   A bottle of milk that is creamy and white!
So cuddle me close, and cuddle me fast,
   And cuddle me snug in my cradle away,
For I hunger and thirst for that precious
   repast —
   Heigh-ho for a bottle, I say!

Lady. Button-Eyes.

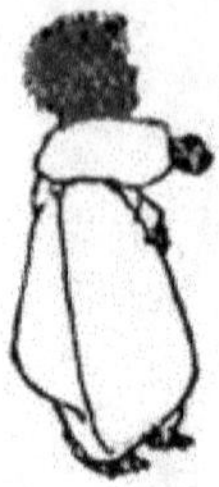

LADY·BUTTON·EYES

WHEN the busy day is done,
And my weary little one
73

Rocketh gently to and fro;
When the night winds softly blow,
And the crickets in the glen
Chirp and chirp and chirp again;
When upon the haunted green
Fairies dance around their queen —
Then from yonder misty skies
Cometh Lady Button-Eyes

Through the murk and mist and gloam
To our quiet, cozy home,
Where to singing, sweet and low,
Rocks a cradle to and fro;
Where the clock's dull monotone
Telleth of the day that 's done;
Where the moonbeams hover o'er
Playthings sleeping on the floor —
Where my weary wee one lies
Cometh Lady Button-Eyes.

Cometh like a fleeting ghost
From some distant eerie coast;
Never footfall can you hear
As that spirit fareth near —

"THEN FROM YONDER MISTY SKIES
COMETH LADY BUTTON-EYES"

LADY BUTTON-EYES

Never whisper, never word
From that shadow-queen is heard.
In ethereal raiment dight,
From the realm of fay and sprite
In the depth of yonder skies
Cometh Lady Button-Eyes.

Layeth she her hands upon
My dear weary little one,
And those white hands overspread
Like a veil the curly head,
Seem to fondle and caress
Every little silken tress;
Then she smooths the eyelids down
Over those two eyes of brown —
In such soothing, tender wise
Cometh Lady Button-Eyes.

Dearest, feel upon your brow
That caressing magic now;
For the crickets in the glen
Chirp and chirp and chirp again,
While upon the haunted green
Fairies dance around their queen,

And the moonbeams hover o'er
Playthings sleeping on the floor —
Hush, my sweet! from yonder skies
Cometh Lady Button-Eyes!

The Ride
to Bumpville.

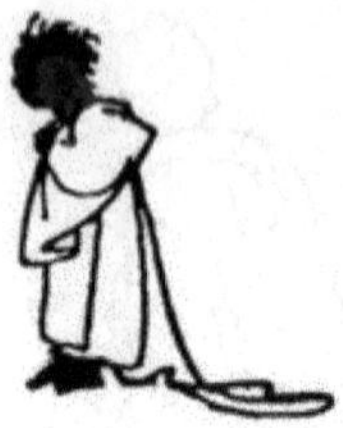

THE RIDE
TO BUMPVILLE.

P LAY that my knee was a calico mare
    Saddled and bridled for Bumpville;
Leap to the back of this steed if you dare,
And gallop away to Bumpville!

81   6

THE RIDE TO BUMPVILLE

I hope you'll be sure to sit fast in your seat,
For this calico mare is prodigiously fleet,
And many adventures you're likely to meet
As you journey along to Bumpville.

This calico mare both gallops and trots
  While whisking you off to Bumpville;
She paces, she shies, and she stumbles, in spots,
  In the tortuous road to Bumpville;
And sometimes this strangely mercurial steed
Will suddenly stop and refuse to proceed,
Which, all will admit, is vexatious indeed,
  When one is *en route* to Bumpville!

THE RIDE TO BUMPVILLE

She's scared of the cars when the engine goes
    " Toot! "
Down by the crossing at Bumpville;
You'd better look out for that treacherous brute
    Bearing you off to Bumpville!
With a snort she rears up on her hindermost
    heels,
And executes jigs and Virginia reels —
Words fail to explain how embarrassed one feels
    Dancing so wildly to Bumpville!

It's bumpytybump and it's jiggityjog,
    Journeying on to Bumpville;
It's over the hilltop and down through the bog
    You ride on your way to Bumpville;
It's rattletybang over boulder and stump,
There are rivers to ford, there are fences to jump,
And the corduroy road it goes bumpytybump,
    Mile after mile to Bumpville!

Perhaps you'll observe it's no easy thing
    Making the journey to Bumpville,
So I think, on the whole, it were prudent to bring
    An end to this ride to Bumpville;

For, though she has uttered no protest or plaint,
The calico mare must be blowing and faint —
What's more to the point, I'm blowed if I ain't!
  So play we have got to Bumpville!

Shuffle-Shoon
and Amber-Locks

SHUFFLE-SHOON AND AMBER-LOCKS

SHUFFLE-SHOON and Amber-Locks
  Sit together, building blocks ;
Shuffle-Shoon is old and grey,
  Amber-Locks a little child,
But together at their play
  Age and Youth are reconciled,
And with sympathetic glee
Build their castles fair to see.

87

" When I grow to be a man "
(So the wee one's prattle ran),
   " I shall build a castle so —
     With a gateway broad and grand;

Here a pretty vine shall grow,
   There a soldier guard shall stand;
And the tower shall be so high,
Folks will wonder, by-and-by ! "

Shuffle-Shoon quoth: " Yes, I know;
Thus I builded long ago!
  Here a gate and there a wall,
    Here a window, there a door:

Here a steeple wondrous tall
  Riseth ever more and more!
But the years have levelled low
What I builded long ago!"

So they gossip at their play,
Heedless of the fleeting day;
  One speaks of the Long Ago
    Where his dead hopes buried lie;
  One with chubby cheeks aglow
    Prattleth of the By-and-By;
Side by side, they build their blocks —
Shuffle-Shoon and Amber-Locks.

The Shut-Eye Train.

THE SHUT-EYE TRAIN.

COME, my little one, with me!
    There are wondrous sights to see

THE SHUT-EYE TRAIN

As the evening shadows fall;
In your pretty cap and gown,
    Don't detain
    The Shut-Eye train —
" Ting-a-ling! " the bell it goeth,
" Toot-toot! " the whistle bloweth,
And we hear the warning call:
" *All aboard for Shut-Eye Town!* "

Over hill and over plain
Soon will speed the Shut-Eye train !
  Through the blue where bloom the stars
  And the Mother Moon looks down
    We'll away
    To land of Fay —
  Oh, the sights that we shall see there!
  Come, my little one, with me there —
'Tis a goodly train of cars —
All aboard for Shut-Eye Town!

Swifter than a wild bird's flight,
Through the realms of fleecy light
  We shall speed and speed away!
  Let the Night in envy frown —

THE SHUT-EYE TRAIN

What care we
How wroth she be!

"TO THE BALOW-FOLK WHO LOVE US"

To the Balow-land above us,
To the Balow-folk who love us,
Let us hasten while we may —
All aboard for Shut-Eye Town!
95

THE SHUT-EYE TRAIN

Shut-Eye Town is passing fair —
Golden dreams await us there;
 We shall dream those dreams, my dear,
 Till the Mother Moon goes down —
   See unfold
    Delights untold!
 And in those mysterious places
 We shall see beloved faces

And beloved voices hear
In the grace of Shut-Eye Town.

Heavy are your eyes, my sweet,
Weary are your little feet —
   Nestle closer up to me
   In your pretty cap and gown;
      Don't detain
      The Shut-Eye train!
  " Ting-a-ling!" the bell it goeth,
  " Toot-toot!" the whistle bloweth;
Oh, the sights that we shall see!
All aboard for Shut-Eye Town!

Little
Oh-Dear.

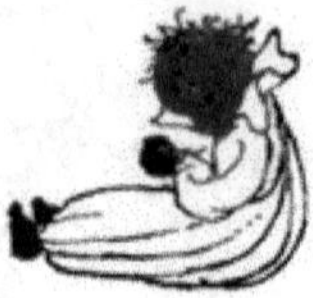

LITTLE·OH·DEAR·

SEE, what a wonderful garden is here,
Planted and trimmed for my Little-Oh-Dear!

LITTLE-OH-DEAR

Posies so gaudy and grass of such brown —
Search ye the country and hunt ye the town
And never ye'll meet with a garden so queer
As this one I've made for my Little-Oh-Dear!

Marigolds white and buttercups blue,
Lilies all dabbled with honey and dew,
The cactus that trails over trellis and wall,
Roses and pansies and violets — all
Make proper obeisance and reverent cheer
When into her garden steps Little-Oh-Dear!

And up at the top of that lavender-tree
A silver-bird singeth as only can she;
For, ever and only, she singeth the song
"I love you — I love you!" the happy day long; —
Then the echo — the echo that smiteth me here!
"I love you, I love you," my Little-Oh-Dear!

The garden may wither, the silver-bird fly —
But what careth my little precious, or I?

"A SILVER-BIRD SINGETH
AS ONLY CAN SHE"

From her pathway of flowers that in spring-time
    upstart
She walketh the tenderer way in my heart;
And, oh, it is always the summer-time *here*
With that song of "I love you," my Little-Oh-
    Dear!

The
Fly·Away Horse.

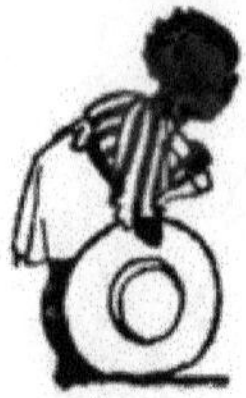

THE FLY-AWAY HORSE.

OH, a wonderful horse is the Fly-Away
  Horse—
  Perhaps you have seen him before;
Perhaps, while you slept, his shadow has swept
  Through the moonlight that floats on the floor.

107

For it's only at night, when the stars twinkle .
    bright,
   That the Fly-Away Horse, with a neigh
And a pull at his rein and a toss of his mane,
    Is up on his heels and away!
        The Moon in the sky,
        As he gallopeth by,
    Cries: "Oh! what a marvellous sight!"
        And the Stars in dismay
        Hide their faces away
   In the lap of old Grandmother Night.

It is yonder, out yonder, the Fly-Away Horse
   Speedeth ever and ever away —
Over meadows and lanes, over mountains and
    plains,
   Over streamlets that sing at their play;
And over the sea like a ghost sweepeth he,
   While the ships they go sailing below,
And he speedeth so fast that the men at the mast
   Adjudge him some portent of woe.
      "What ho there!" they cry,
      As he flourishes by

"THE MOON IN THE SKY,
AS HE GALLOPETH BY,
CRIES: 'OH! WHAT A MARVELLOUS SIGHT!'"

THE FLY-AWAY HORSE

With a whisk of his beautiful tail;
And the fish in the sea
Are as scared as can be,
From the nautilus up to the whale!

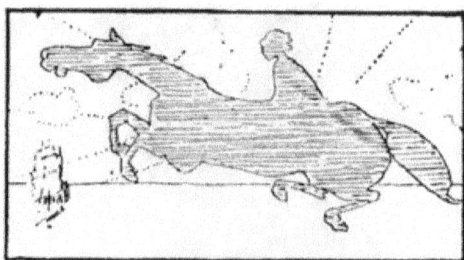

And the Fly-Away Horse seeks those far-away
lands
You little folk dream of at night —
Where candy-trees grow, and honey-brooks flow,
And corn-fields with popcorn are white;
And the beasts in the wood are ever so good
To children who visit them there —
What glory astride of a lion to ride,
Or to wrestle around with a bear!
The monkeys, they say:
" Come on, let us play,"

And they frisk in the cocoa-nut trees:
  While the parrots, that cling
  To the peanut-vines, sing
Or converse with comparative ease!

Off! scamper to bed — you shall ride him to-night!
  For, as soon as you've fallen asleep,
With a jubilant neigh he shall bear you away
  Over forest and hillside and deep!
But tell us, my dear, all you see and you hear
  In those beautiful lands over there,
Where the Fly-Away Horse wings his far-away
    course
  With the wee one consigned to his care.
      Then grandma will cry
      In amazement: " Oh, my! "

And she'll think it could never be so;
  And only we two
  Shall know it is true —
You and I, little precious! shall know!

Fiddle-Dee-Dee.

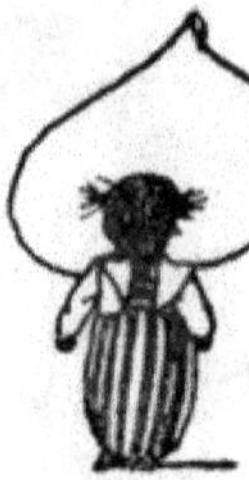

FIDDLE-DEE-DEE.

THERE once was a bird that lived up in a
    tree,
And all he could whistle was " Fiddle-dee-dee "—
A very provoking, unmusical song
For one to be whistling the summer day long!
Yet always contented and busy was he
With that vocal recurrence of " Fiddle-dee-dee."

Hard by lived a brave little soldier of four,
That weird iteration repented him sore;

'By
our St Didy!
the deed
must be done'

FIDDLE-DEE-DEE

" I prithee, Dear-Mother-Mine! fetch me my
    gun,
For, by our St. Didy! the deed must be done
That shall presently rid all creation and me
Of that ominous bird and his ' Fiddle-dee-dee'! "

Then out came Dear-Mother-Mine, bringing her
    son
His awfully truculent little red gun;
The stock was of pine and the barrel of tin,
The " bang" it came out where the bullet went
    in —
The right kind of weapon I think you'll agree
For slaying all fowl that go " Fiddle-dee-dee"!

The brave little soldier quoth never a word,
But he up and he drew a straight bead on that
    bird;
And, while that vain creature provokingly sang,
The gun it went off with a terrible bang!

Then loud laughed the youth — "By my Bottle,"
    cried he,
"I've put a quietus on ' Fiddle-dee-dee'!"

'The
   "bang" it came out
   where the
    bullet went in-'

Out came then Dear-Mother-Mine, saying: "My
son,

'"By
my Bottle"
cried he,'

Right well have you wrought with your little red
    gun !
Hereafter no evil at all need I fear,
With such a brave soldier as You-My-Love here!"
She kissed the dear boy.

               [The bird in the tree
Continued to whistle his " Fiddle-dee-dee "!]

POEMS FROM " WITH TRUMPET AND DRUM."

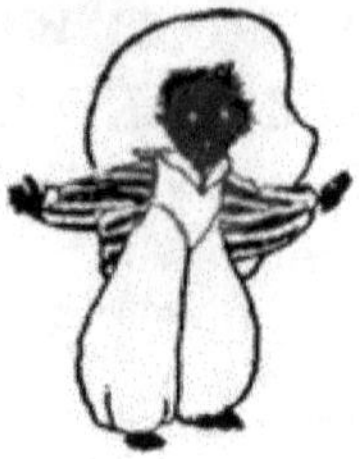

The
Sugar Plum Tree.

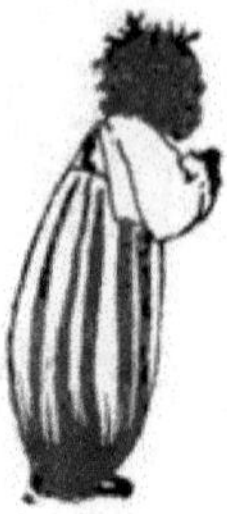

THE SUGAR- -PLUM TREE..

HAVE you ever heard of the Sugar-Plum
Tree?
'Tis a marvel of great renown!

125

It blooms on the shore of the Lollipop sea
In the garden of Shut-Eye Town;

When
    you've got to
        the tree,

THE SUGAR-PLUM TREE

The fruit that it bears is so wondrously sweet
(As those who have tasted it say)

That good little children have only to eat
Of that fruit to be happy next day.

THE SUGAR-PLUM TREE

When you've got to the tree, you would have a
    hard time
  To capture the fruit which I sing;
The tree is so tall that no person could climb
  To the boughs where the sugar-plums swing!
But up in that tree sits a chocolate cat,
  And a gingerbread dog prowls below —
And this is the way you contrive to get at
  Those sugar-plums tempting you so:

You say but the word to that gingerbread dog
  And he barks with such terrible zest
That the chocolate cat is at once all agog,
  As her swelling proportions attest.
And the chocolate cat goes cavorting around
  From this leafy limb unto that,
And the sugar-plums tumble, of course, to the
    ground —
  Hurrah for that chocolate cat!

There are marshmallows, gumdrops, and pepper-
    mint canes,
  With stripings of scarlet or gold,
And you carry away of the treasure that rains
  As much as your apron can hold!

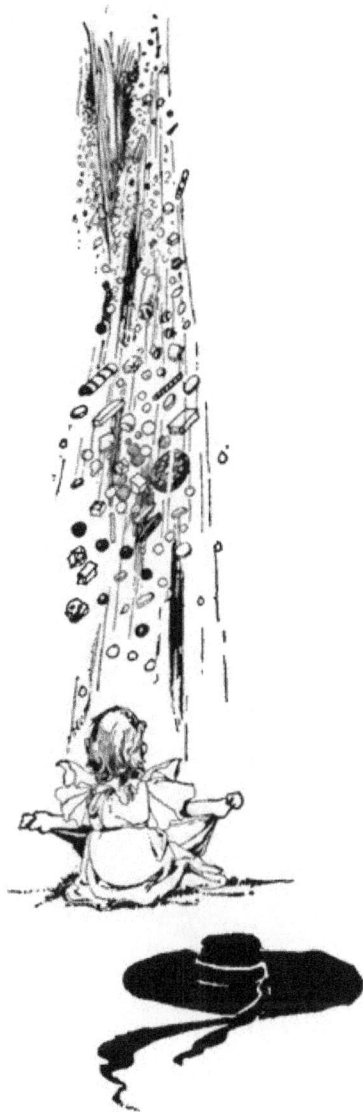

"AS MUCH AS YOUR APRON CAN HOLD!"

So come, little child, cuddle closer to me
  In your dainty white nightcap and gown,
And I'll rock you away to that Sugar-Plum Tree
  In the garden of Shut-Eye Town.

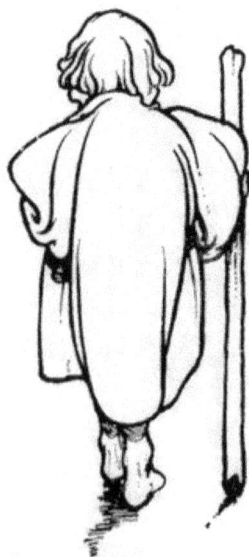

Krinken.

KRINKEN.

KRINKEN was a little child, —
It was summer when he smiled,

KRINKEN

Oft the hoary sea and grim
Stretched its white arms out to him;
Calling, " Sun-child, come to me;
Let me warm my heart with thee! "
But the child heard not the sea.

Krinken on the beach one day
Saw a maiden Nis at play;
Fair, and very fair, was she,
Just a little child was he.
" Krinken," said the maiden Nis,
" Let me have a little kiss, —
Just a kiss, and go with me
To the summer-lands that be
Down within the silver sea."

Krinken was a little child,
By the maiden Nis beguiled;
Down into the calling sea
With the maiden Nis went he.

But the sea calls out no more,
It is winter on the shore, —

KRINKEN

Winter where that little child
Made sweet summer when he smiled;
Though 'tis summer on the sea
Where with maiden Nis went he, —
Summer, summer evermore, —
It is winter on the shore,
Winter, winter evermore.

Of the summer on the deep
Come sweet visions in my sleep;
His fair face lifts from the sea,
His dear voice calls out to me, —
These my dreams of summer be.

Krinken was a little child,
By the maiden Nis beguiled;
Oft the hoary sea and grim
Reached its longing arms to him,
Crying, " Sun-child, come to me;
Let me warm my heart with thee! "
But the sea calls out no more;
It is winter on the shore, —
Winter, cold and dark and wild;
Krinken was a little child, —

KRINKEN

It was summer when he smiled;
Down he went into the sea,
And the winter bides with me.
Just a little child was ho.

Pittypat
and Tippytoe.

PITTYPAT-
AND
TIPPYTOE.

A LL day long they come and go —
    Pittypat and Tippytoe;
Footprints up and down the hall,
    Playthings scattered on the floor,

139

'Only
buttered bread
will do,'

'Inches
thick with
sugar too.'

PITTYPAT AND TIPPYTOE

Finger-marks along the wall,
　　Tell-tale smudges on the door —
By these presents you shall know
Pittypat and Tippytoe.

How they riot at their play!
And a dozen times a day
　　In they troop, demanding bread —
　　　Only buttered bread will do,
　　And the butter must be spread
　　　Inches thick with sugar too!
And I never can say "No,
Pittypat and Tippytoe!"

Sometimes there are griefs to soothe,
Sometimes ruffled brows to smooth;
　　For (I much regret to say)
　　　Tippytoe and Pittypat
　　Sometimes interrupt their play
　　　With an internecine spat;
Fie, for shame! to quarrel so —
Pittypat and Tippytoe!

142

PITTYPAT AND TIPPYTOE

Oh the thousand worrying things
Every day recurrent brings!
  Hands to scrub and hair to brush,
    Search for playthings gone amiss,
  Many a wee complaint to hush,
    Many a little bump to kiss;
Life seems one vain, fleeting show
To Pittypat and Tippytoe!

And when day is at an end,
There are little duds to mend:
  Little frocks are strangely torn,
    Little shoes great holes reveal,
  Little hose, but one day worn,
    Rudely yawn at toe and heel!
Who but *you* could work such woe,
Pittypat and Tippytoe!

On the floor and down the hall,
Rudely smutched upon the wall,
  There are proofs in every kind
    Of the havoc they have wrought,

PITTYPAT AND TIPPYTOE

And upon my heart you'd find
    Just such trade-marks, if you sought;
Oh, how glad I am 'tis so,
Pittypat and Tippytoe!

Little Blue Pigeon.

LITTLE BLUE PIGEON.

SLEEP, little pigeon, and fold your wings —
    Little blue pigeon with velvet eyes;

147

Sleep to the singing of mother-bird swinging —
  Swinging the nest where her little one lies.

Away out yonder I see a star —
  Silvery star with a tinkling song;
To the soft dew falling I hear it calling —
  Calling and tinkling the night along.

In through the window a moonbeam comes —
  Little gold moonbeam with misty wings;
All silently creeping, it asks: " Is he sleeping —
  Sleeping and dreaming while mother sings?"

Up from the sea there floats the sob
  Of the waves that are breaking upon the shore.
As though they were groaning in anguish, and
    moaning —
  Bemoaning the ship that shall come no more.

But sleep, little pigeon, and fold your wings —
Little blue pigeon with mournful eyes;
Am I not singing? — see, I am swinging —
Swinging the nest where my darling lies.

Teeny-Weeny.

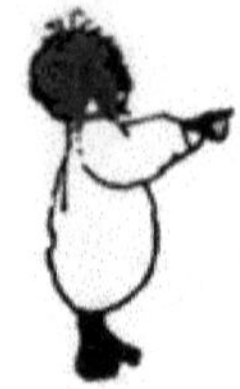

TEENY-WEENY.

E VERY evening, after tea,
  Teeny-Weeny comes to me.

TEENY-WEENY

And, astride my willing knee,
  Plies his lash and rides away;
Though that palfrey, all too spare,
Finds his burden hard to bear,
Teeny-Weeny doesn't care;
  He commands, and I obey!

First it's trot, and gallop then;
Now it's back to trot again;
Teeny-Weeny likes it when
  He is riding fierce and fast.
Then his dark eyes brighter grow
And his cheeks are all aglow:
" More! " he cries, and never " Whoa! "
  Till the horse breaks down at last.

Oh, the strange and lovely sights
Teeny-Weeny sees of nights,
As he makes those famous flights
  On that wondrous horse of his!
Oftentimes before he knows,
Wearylike his eyelids close,

And, still smiling, off he goes
  Where the land of By-low is.

There he sees the folk of fay
Hard at ring-a-rosie play,
And he hears those fairies say:
  "Come, let's chase him to and fro!"
But, with a defiant shout,
Teeny puts that host to rout;
Of this tale I make no doubt,
  Every night he tells it so.

So I feel a tender pride
In my boy who dares to ride

TEENY-WEENY

That fierce horse of his astride,
  Off into those misty lands;

And as on my breast he lies,
Dreaming in that wondrous wise,
I caress his folded eyes,
  Pat his little dimpled hands.

On a time he went away,
Just a little while to stay,
And I'm not ashamed to say
  I was very lonely then;
Life without him was so sad,
You can fancy I was glad

TEENY-WEENY

And made merry when I had
  Teeny-Weeny back again!

So of evenings, after tea,
When he toddles up to me
And goes tugging at my knee,
  You should hear his palfrey neigh!
You should see him prance and shy,
When, with an exulting cry,
Teeny-Weeny, vaulting high,
  Plies his lash and rides away!

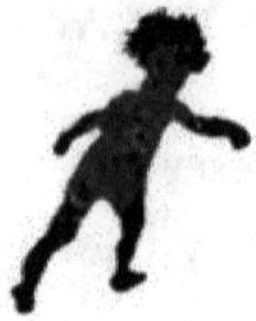

Buttercup, Poppy,
        Forget-me-not.

BUTTERCUP,
POPPY, FOR-
GET-ME-NOT.

B UTTERCUP, Poppy, Forget-me-not —
These three bloomed in a garden spot;

BUTTERCUP, POPPY, FORGET-ME-NOT

And once, all merry with song and play,
A little one heard three voices say :
   " Shine and shadow, summer and spring,
     O thou child with the tangled hair
   And laughing eyes ! we three shall bring
     Each an offering passing fair."
The little one did not understand,
But they bent and kissed the dimpled hand.

Buttercup gamboled all day long,
Sharing the little one's mirth and song ;
Then, stealing along on misty gleams,
Poppy came bearing the sweetest dreams.
   Playing and dreaming — and that was all
     Till once a sleeper would not awake ;
   Kissing the little face under the pall,
     We thought of the words the third flower
       spake ;
And we found betimes in a hallowed spot
The solace and peace of Forget-me-not.

Buttercup shareth the joy of day,
Glinting with gold the hours of play ;
Bringeth the poppy sweet repose,
When the hands would fold and the eyes would
   close ;

And after it all — the play and the sleep
   Of a little life — what cometh then?
To the hearts that ache and the eyes that weep
   A new flower bringeth God's peace again.
Each one serveth its tender lot —
Buttercup, Poppy, Forget-me-not.

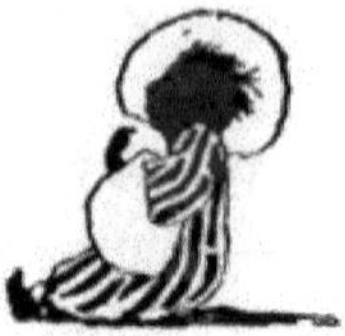

Wynken, Blynken, and Nod.

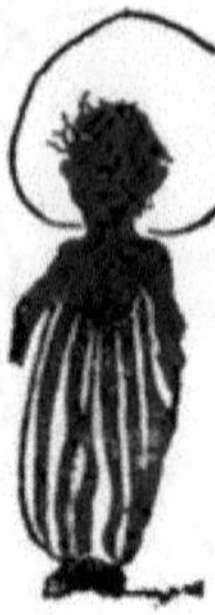

WYNKEN, BLYNKEN, AND NOD.

WYNKEN, Blynken, and Nod one night
    Sailed off in a wooden shoe —
Sailed on a river of crystal light,
    Into a sea of dew.

" Where are you going, and what do you wish?"
The old moon asked the three.
" We have come to fish for the herring fish
That live in this beautiful sea;
Nets of silver and gold have we!"
                    Said Wynken,
                    Blynken,
                    And Nod.

The old moon laughed and sang a song,
    As they rocked in the wooden shoe,
And the wind that sped them all night long
    Ruffled the waves of dew.
The little stars were the herring fish
    That lived in that beautiful sea —
" Now cast your nets wherever you wish —
    Never afeard are we ";
    So cried the stars to the fishermen three:
                    Wynken,
                    Blynken,
                    And Nod.

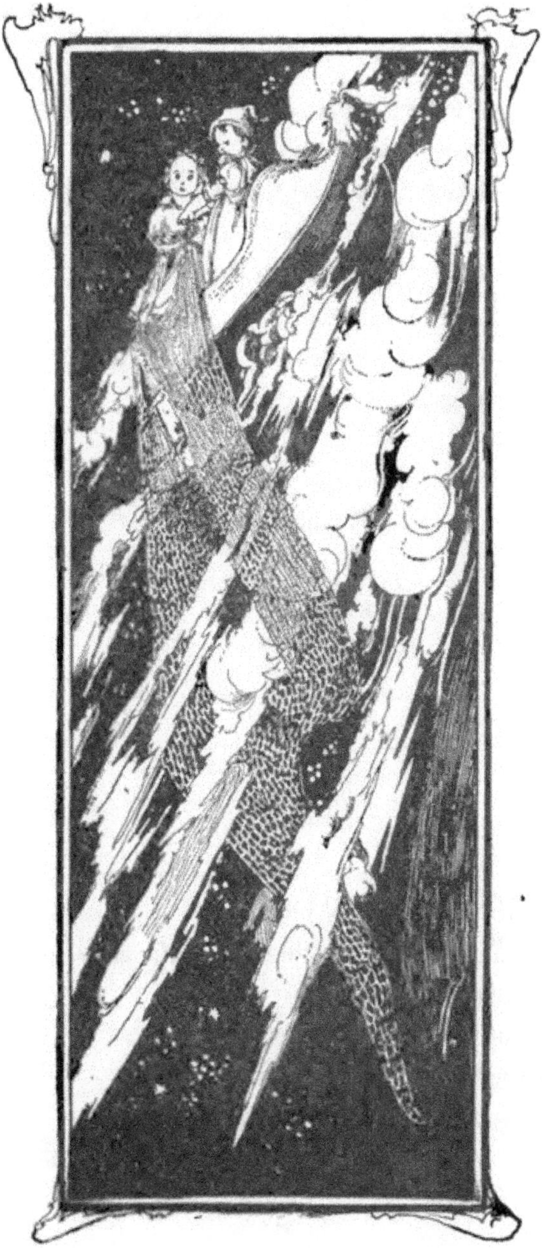

All night long their nets they threw
  To the stars in the twinkling foam —
Then down from the skies came the wooden shoe,
  Bringing the fishermen home;
'Twas all so pretty a sail it seemed
  As if it could not be,
And some folks thought 'twas a dream they'd
    dreamed
  Of sailing that beautiful sea —
  But I shall name you the fishermen three:
          Wynken,
          Blynken,
          And Nod.

Wynken and Blynken are two little eyes,
  And Nod is a little head,
And the wooden shoe that sailed the skies
  Is a wee one's trundle-bed.
So shut your eyes while mother sings
  Of wonderful sights that be,
And you shall see the beautiful things

WYNKEN, BLYNKEN, AND NOD

As you rock in the misty sea,
Where the old shoe rocked the fishermen three:
Wynken,
Blynken,
And Nod.

Little Mistress Sans-Merci.

LITTLE MISTRESS SANS-MERCI.

L ITTLE Mistress Sans-Merci
    Fareth world-wide, fancy free:

175

Trotteth cooing to and fro,
    And her cooing is command —
Never ruled there yet, I trow,
    Mightier despot in the land.
And my heart it lieth where
Mistress Sans-Merci doth fare.

Little Mistress Sans-Merci —
She hath made a slave of me!
    "Go," she biddeth, and I go —
      "Come," and I am fain to come —

Never mercy doth she show,
  Be she wroth or frolicsome,
Yet am I content to be
Slave to Mistress Sans-Merci!

Little Mistress Sans-Merci
Hath become so dear to me
  That I count as passing sweet
    All the pain her moods impart,
  And I bless the little feet
    That go trampling on my heart:
Ah, how lonely life would be
But for little Sans-Merci!

Little Mistress Sans-Merci,
Cuddle close this night to me,
  And the heart, which all day long
    Ruthless thou hast trod upon,

Shall outpour a soothing song
For its best belovèd one —
All its tenderness for thee,
Little Mistress Sans-Merci!

Hi-Spy.

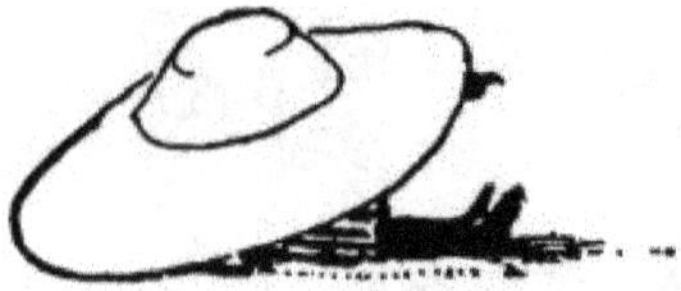

HI-SPY.

STRANGE that the city thoroughfare,
   Noisy and bustling all the day,
Should with the night renounce its care
   And lend itself to children's play!

Oh, girls are girls, and boys are boys,
   And have been so since Abel's birth,
And shall be so till dolls and toys
   Are with the children swept from earth.

181

The selfsame sport that crowns the day
  Of many a Syrian shepherd's son,
Beguiles the little lads at play
  By night in stately Babylon.

I hear their voices in the street,
  Yet 'tis so different now from then!
Come, brother! from your winding-sheet,
  And let us two be boys again!

Little Boy Blue.

LITTLE BOY BLUE.

THE little toy dog is covered with dust,
    But sturdy and stanch he stands;
And the little toy soldier is red with rust,
   And the musket moulds in his hands.

185

LITTLE BOY BLUE

Time was when the little toy dog was new,
    And the soldier was passing fair;
And that was the time when our Little Boy Blue
    Kissed them and put them there.

" Now, don't you go till I come," he said,
    " And don't you make any noise!"
So, toddling off to his trundle-bed,
    He dreamt of the pretty toys;
And, as he was dreaming, an angel song
    Awakened our Little Boy Blue —
Oh! the years are many, the years are long,
    But the little toy friends are true!

Aye, faithful to Little Boy Blue they stand,
    Each in the same old place —
Awaiting the touch of a little hand,
    The smile of a little face;

And they wonder, as waiting the long years
   through
In the dust of that little chair,
What has become of our Little Boy Blue,
   Since he kissed them and put them there.

Heigho, My Dearie

HEIGHO, MY DEARIE

A MOONBEAM floateth from the skies,
  Whispering: "Heigho, my dearie;

191

HEIGHO, MY DEARIE

I would spin a web before your eyes —
A beautiful web of silver light
Wherein is many a wondrous sight
Of a radiant garden leagues away,
Where the softly tinkling lilies sway
And the snow-white lambkins are at play —
    Heigho, my dearie! "

A brownie stealeth from the vine,
    Singing: " Heigho, my dearie;
And will you hear this song of mine —
A song of the land of murk and mist
Where bideth the bud the dew hath kist?
Then let the moonbeam's web of light
Be spun before thee silvery white,
And I shall sing the livelong night —
    Heigho, my dearie! "

The night wind speedeth from the sea,
    Murmuring: " Heigho, my dearie;
I bring a mariner's prayer for thee;
So let the moonbeam veil thine eyes,
And the brownie sing thee lullabies —

But I shall rock thee to and fro,
Kissing the brow *he* loveth so.
And the prayer shall guard thy bed, I trow —
    Heigho, my dearie!"

Fairy and Child.

FAIRY AND CHILD.

OH, listen, little Dear-My-Soul,
  To the fairy voices calling,
197

For the moon is high in the misty sky
  And the honey dew is falling;
To the midnight feast in the clover bloom
  The bluebells are a-ringing,
And it's " Come away to the land of fay "
  That the katydid is singing.

Oh, slumber, little Dear-My-Soul,
  And hand in hand we'll wander —
Hand in hand to the beautiful land
  Of Balow, away off yonder;
Or we'll sail along in a lily leaf
  Into the white moon's halo —
Over a stream of mist and dream
  Into the land of Balow.

Or, you shall have two beautiful wings —
  Two gossamer wings and airy,
And all the while shall the old moon smile
  And think you a little fairy;

"INTO THE WHITE MOON'S HALO"

FAIRY AND CHILD

And you shall dance in the velvet sky,
  And the silvery stars shall twinkle
And dream sweet dreams as over their beams
  Your footfalls softly tinkle.

Child and Mother.

CHILD AND MOTHER

O MOTHER-MY-LOVE, if you'll give me your hand,
And go where I ask you to wander,

CHILD AND MOTHER

I will lead you away to a beautiful land —
  The Dreamland that's waiting out yonder.
We'll walk in a sweet-posie garden out there,
  Where moonlight and starlight are streaming,
And the flowers and the birds are filling the air
  With the fragrance and music of dreaming.

There'll be no little tired-out boy to undress,
  No questions or cares to perplex you;
There'll be no little bruises or bumps to caress,
  Nor patching of stockings to vex you.
For I'll rock you away on a silver-dew stream,
  And sing you asleep when you're weary,
And no one shall know of our beautiful dream,
  But you and your own little dearie.

And when I am tired I'll nestle my head
  In the bosom that's soothed me so often,
And the wide-awake stars shall sing in my stead
  A song which our dreaming shall soften.

CHILD AND MOTHER

So, Mother-My-Love, let me take your dear hand,
  And away through the starlight we'll wander —
Away through the mist to the beautiful land —
  The Dreamland that's waiting out yonder.

Canderfeather's Gift.

GANDERFEATHER'S GIFT

I WAS just a little thing
   When a fairy came and kissed me;

14

GANDERFEATHER'S GIFT

Floating in upon the light
Of a haunted summer night,
Lo, the fairies came to sing
Pretty slumber songs and bring
    Certain boons that else had missed me.
From a dream I turned to see
What those strangers brought for me,
    When that fairy up and kissed me —
    Here, upon this cheek, he kissed me!

Simmerdew was there, but she
    Did not like me altogether;
Daisybright and Turtledove,
Pilfercurds and Honeylove,
Thistleblow and Amberglee
On that gleaming, ghostly sea
    Floated from the misty heather,
And around my trundle-bed
Frisked, and looked, and whispering said —
    Solemnlike and all together:
" *You* shall kiss him, Ganderfeather!"

Ganderfeather kissed me then —
    Ganderfeather, quaint and merry!

210

GANDERFEATHER'S GIFT

No attenuate sprite was he,
— But as buxom as could be; —
Kissed me twice, and once again,
And the others shouted when

On my cheek uprose a berry
Somewhat like a mole, mayhap,
But the kiss-mark of that chap
    Ganderfeather, passing merry —
    Humorsome, but kindly, very!

I was just a tiny thing
    When the prankish Ganderfeather

Brought this curious gift to me
With his fairy kisses three;
Yet with honest pride I sing
That same gift he chose to bring
 Out of yonder haunted heather.
Other charms and friendships fly —
Constant friends this mole and I,
 Who have been so long together.
 Thank you, little Ganderfeather!

FROM THE SECOND BOOK OF VERSE

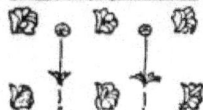

Telling the Bees

TELLING THE BEES. 219

OUT of the house where the slumberer lay
Grandfather came one summer day,

And under the pleasant orchard trees
He spake this wise to the murmuring bees:
    " The clover-bloom that kissed her feet
    And the posie-bed where she used to play,
    Have honey store, but none so sweet
    As ere our little one went away.
    O bees, sing soft, and, bees, sing low;
    For she is gone who loved you so."

A wonder fell on the listening bees
Under those pleasant orchard trees,
And in their toil that summer day
Ever their murmuring seemed to say:
    " Child, O child, the grass is cool,
    And the posies are waking to hear the song
    Of the bird that swings by the shaded pool,
    Waiting for one that tarrieth long."
    'Twas so they called to the little one then,
    As if to call her back again.

O gentle bees, I have come to say
That grandfather fell asleep to-day,

TELLING THE BEES

And we know by the smile on grandfather's face
He has found his dear one's biding-place.
   So, bees, sing soft, and, bees, sing low,
   As over the honey-fields you sweep —
   To the trees abloom and the flowers ablow
   Sing of grandfather fast asleep;
  And ever beneath these orchard trees
  Find cheer and shelter, gentle bees.

FROM 'THE LONE-SOME LITTLE SHOE

✳ ✳ ✳ ✳ ✳

Contentment.

CONTENTMENT.

ONCE on a time an old red hen
   Went strutting round with pompous clucks,
For she had little babies ten,
   A part of which were tiny ducks.
" 'Tis very rare that hens," said she,
   " Have baby ducks as well as chicks —
But I possess, as you can see,
   Of chickens four and ducklings six! "

CONTENTMENT

A season later, this old hen
   Appeared, still cackling of her luck,
For, though she boasted babies ten,
   Not one among them was a duck!
" 'Tis well," she murmured, brooding o'er
  The little chicks of fleecy down,
" My babies now will stay ashore,
   And, consequently, cannot drown ! "

The following spring the old red hen
   Clucked just as proudly as of yore. —
But lo! her babes were ducklings ten,
   Instead of chickens as before!
" 'Tis better," said the old red hen,
   As she surveyed her waddling brood;
" A little water now and then
   Will surely do my darlings good ! "

But, oh! alas, how very sad!
  When gentle spring rolled round again,
The eggs eventuated bad,
  And childless was the old red hen!
Yet patiently she bore her woe,
  And still she wore a cheerful air,
And said: " 'Tis best these things are so
  For babies are a dreadful care!"

I half suspect that many men,
  And many, many women, too,
Could learn a lesson from the hen
  With foliage of vermilion hue.
She ne'er presumed to take offence
  At any fate that might befall,
But meekly bowed to Providence. —
  She was contented — that was all!

· THE · END ·

www.ingramcontent.com/pod-product-compliance
Lightning Source LLC
Chambersburg PA
CBHW030316270326
41926CB00010B/1389